The Write Plan

WRITER'S NOTEBOOK
Organize Your Ideas and Start Writing

HANNAH BAUMAN

Between the Lines Editorial
Editing and Coaching for Writers

The secret of
getting ahead
is getting
started.

- Mark Twain

How to Use This Notebook

Hello, writer! Welcome to The Write Plan, a guided notebook for fiction writers.

In this notebook, you'll find:

One (1) unlabeled section for quick notes, tracking your word count, and setting writing goals; and

Six (6) labeled sections to help you organize your ideas for novels and stories

Each labeled section was designed to help you lay out both the basics and more intricate details of your stories. Don't be afraid to get creative in whatever way helps your writing process. The dot grid pages in each section are there for you to use however you see fit, whether that's with doodles, maps, sticky notes, more lists, etc. Remember, there is no wrong way to plan and write your story.

Please note this notebook is not meant to teach you about plotting, character development, or worldbuilding. Instead, it serves as a home for all of your ideas, notes, goals, and accomplishments.

If you're looking for more writing tips, check out my Instagram @blteditorial or visit btleditorial.com/blog for articles and podcast episodes all about writing fiction.

Happy writing!

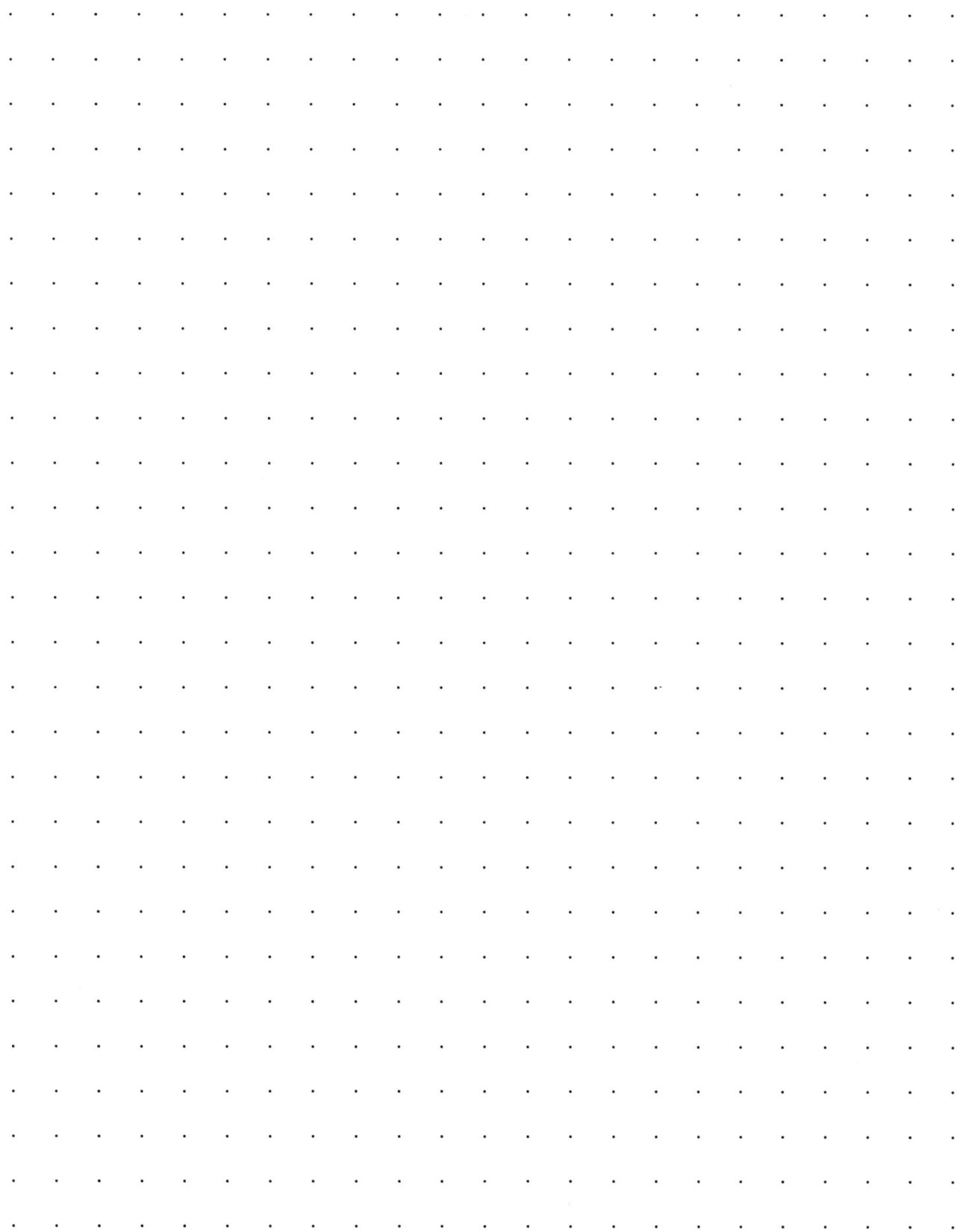

Word Count Tracker

Date	Project	Word Count Added	Word Count Total

Word Count Tracker

Date	Project	Word Count Added	Word Count Total

Word Count Tracker

Date	Project	Word Count Added	Word Count Total

Word Count Tracker

Date	Project	Word Count Added	Word Count Total

Writing Goals: Three Months

Things I want to accomplish in the next three months	
1.	2.
3.	4.

Steps I can take toward these goals:

1.

2.

3.

4.

Writing Goals: Six Months

Things I want to accomplish in the next six months	
1.	2.
3.	4.

Steps I can take toward these goals:

1.

2.

3.

4.

Writing Goals: One Year

Things I want to accomplish in the next year	
1.	2.
3.	4.

Steps I can take toward these goals:

1.

2.

3.

4.

ideas & notes

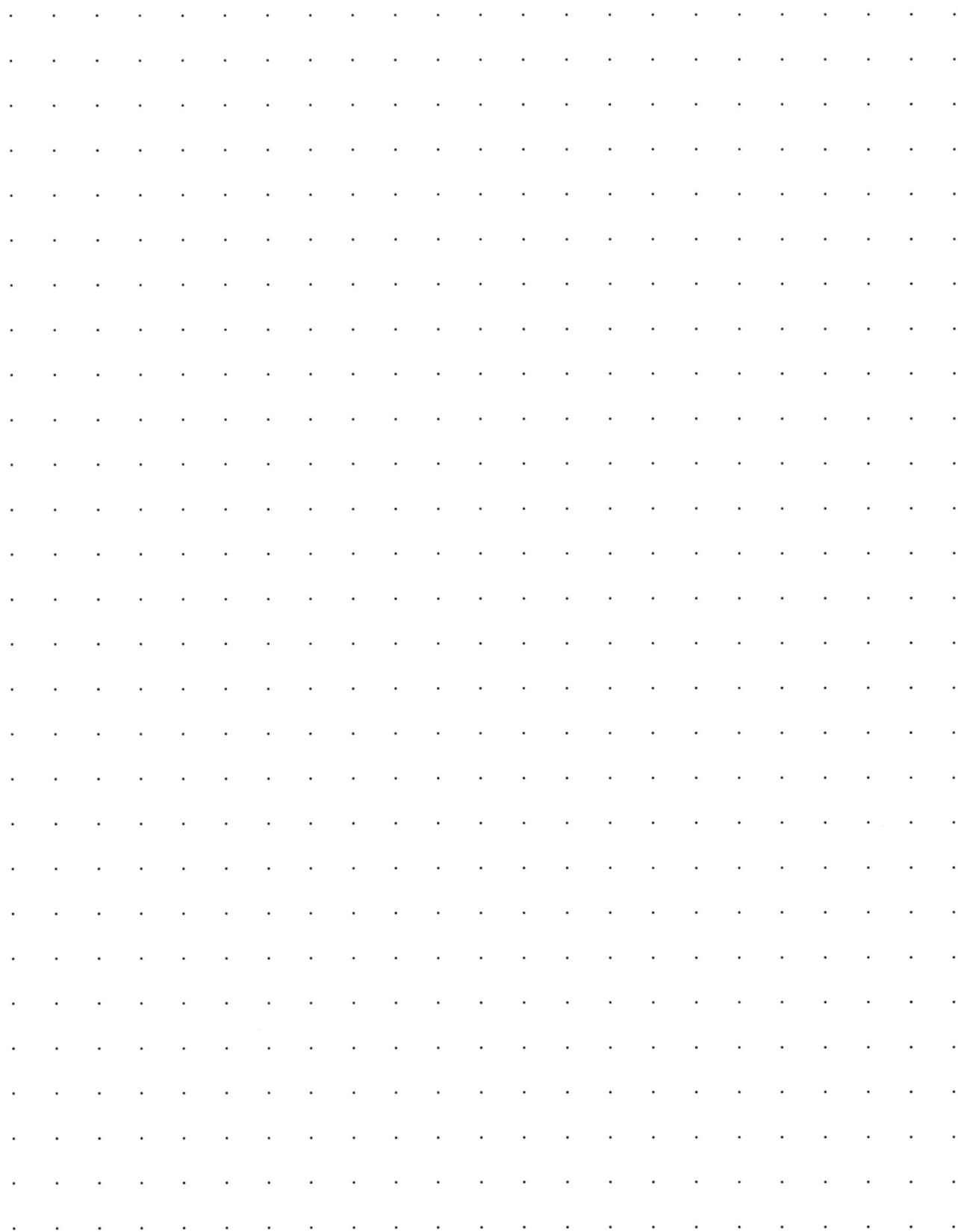

characters

Character List

Name:

Short Description:

- ◯ Main
- ◯ Supporting
- ◯ Recurring
- ◯ Throwaway

Name:

Short Description:

- ◯ Main
- ◯ Supporting
- ◯ Recurring
- ◯ Throwaway

Name:

Short Description:

- ◯ Main
- ◯ Supporting
- ◯ Recurring
- ◯ Throwaway

Name:

Short Description:

- ◯ Main
- ◯ Supporting
- ◯ Recurring
- ◯ Throwaway

Name:

Short Description:

- ◯ Main
- ◯ Supporting
- ◯ Recurring
- ◯ Throwaway

Character List

Name:

Short Description:

- ○ Main
- ○ Supporting
- ○ Recurring
- ○ Throwaway

Name:

Short Description:

- ○ Main
- ○ Supporting
- ○ Recurring
- ○ Throwaway

Name:

Short Description:

- ○ Main
- ○ Supporting
- ○ Recurring
- ○ Throwaway

Name:

Short Description:

- ○ Main
- ○ Supporting
- ○ Recurring
- ○ Throwaway

Name:

Short Description:

- ○ Main
- ○ Supporting
- ○ Recurring
- ○ Throwaway

Character List

Name:

Short Description:

- ○ Main
- ○ Supporting
- ○ Recurring
- ○ Throwaway

Name:

Short Description:

- ○ Main
- ○ Supporting
- ○ Recurring
- ○ Throwaway

Name:

Short Description:

- ○ Main
- ○ Supporting
- ○ Recurring
- ○ Throwaway

Name:

Short Description:

- ○ Main
- ○ Supporting
- ○ Recurring
- ○ Throwaway

Name:

Short Description:

- ○ Main
- ○ Supporting
- ○ Recurring
- ○ Throwaway

Character List

Name:

Short Description:

- ○ Main
- ○ Supporting
- ○ Recurring
- ○ Throwaway

Name:

Short Description:

- ○ Main
- ○ Supporting
- ○ Recurring
- ○ Throwaway

Name:

Short Description:

- ○ Main
- ○ Supporting
- ○ Recurring
- ○ Throwaway

Name:

Short Description:

- ○ Main
- ○ Supporting
- ○ Recurring
- ○ Throwaway

Name:

Short Description:

- ○ Main
- ○ Supporting
- ○ Recurring
- ○ Throwaway

Character Design Sheet

Name:

Nickname/Alias:

Age:

Hair color:

Gender identity:

Physique:

Height:

Skin tone:

Eye color:

Other features:

Habits and quirks:

Goals and motives:

Strengths:

Weaknesses:

Notes:

Character Design Sheet

Name:

Nickname/Alias:

Age:

Hair color:

Gender identity:

Physique:

Height:

Skin tone:

Eye color:

Other features:

Habits and quirks:

Goals and motives:

Strengths:

Weaknesses:

Notes:

Character Design Sheet

Name:

Nickname/Alias:

Age:

Hair color:

Gender identity:

Physique:

Height:

Skin tone:

Eye color:

Other features:

Habits and quirks:

Goals and motives:

Strengths:

Weaknesses:

Notes:

Character Design Sheet

Name:

Nickname/Alias:

Age:

Hair color:

Gender identity:

Physique:

Height:

Skin tone:

Eye color:

Other features:

Habits and quirks:

Goals and motives:

Strengths:

Weaknesses:

Notes:

Character Design Sheet

Name:

Nickname/Alias:

Age:

Hair color:

Gender identity:

Physique:

Height:

Skin tone:

Eye color:

Other features:

Habits and quirks:

Goals and motives:

Strengths:

Weaknesses:

Notes:

Character Design Sheet

Name:

Nickname/Alias:

Age:

Hair color:

Gender identity:

Physique:

Height:

Skin tone:

Eye color:

Other features:

Habits and quirks:

Goals and motives:

Strengths:

Weaknesses:

Notes:

Character Design Sheet

Name:

Nickname/Alias:

Age:

Hair color:

Gender identity:

Physique:

Height:

Skin tone:

Eye color:

Other features:

Habits and quirks:

Goals and motives:

Strengths:

Weaknesses:

Notes:

Character Design Sheet

Name:

Nickname/Alias:

Age: Hair color:

Gender identity: Physique:

Height: Skin tone:

Eye color: Other features:

Habits and quirks:

Goals and motives:

Strengths:

Weaknesses:

Notes:

Character Design Sheet

Name:

Nickname/Alias:

Age:

Hair color:

Gender identity:

Physique:

Height:

Skin tone:

Eye color:

Other features:

Habits and quirks:

Goals and motives:

Strengths:

Weaknesses:

Notes:

Character Design Sheet

Name:

Nickname/Alias:

Age:

Hair color:

Gender identity:

Physique:

Height:

Skin tone:

Eye color:

Other features:

Habits and quirks:

Goals and motives:

Strengths:

Weaknesses:

Notes:

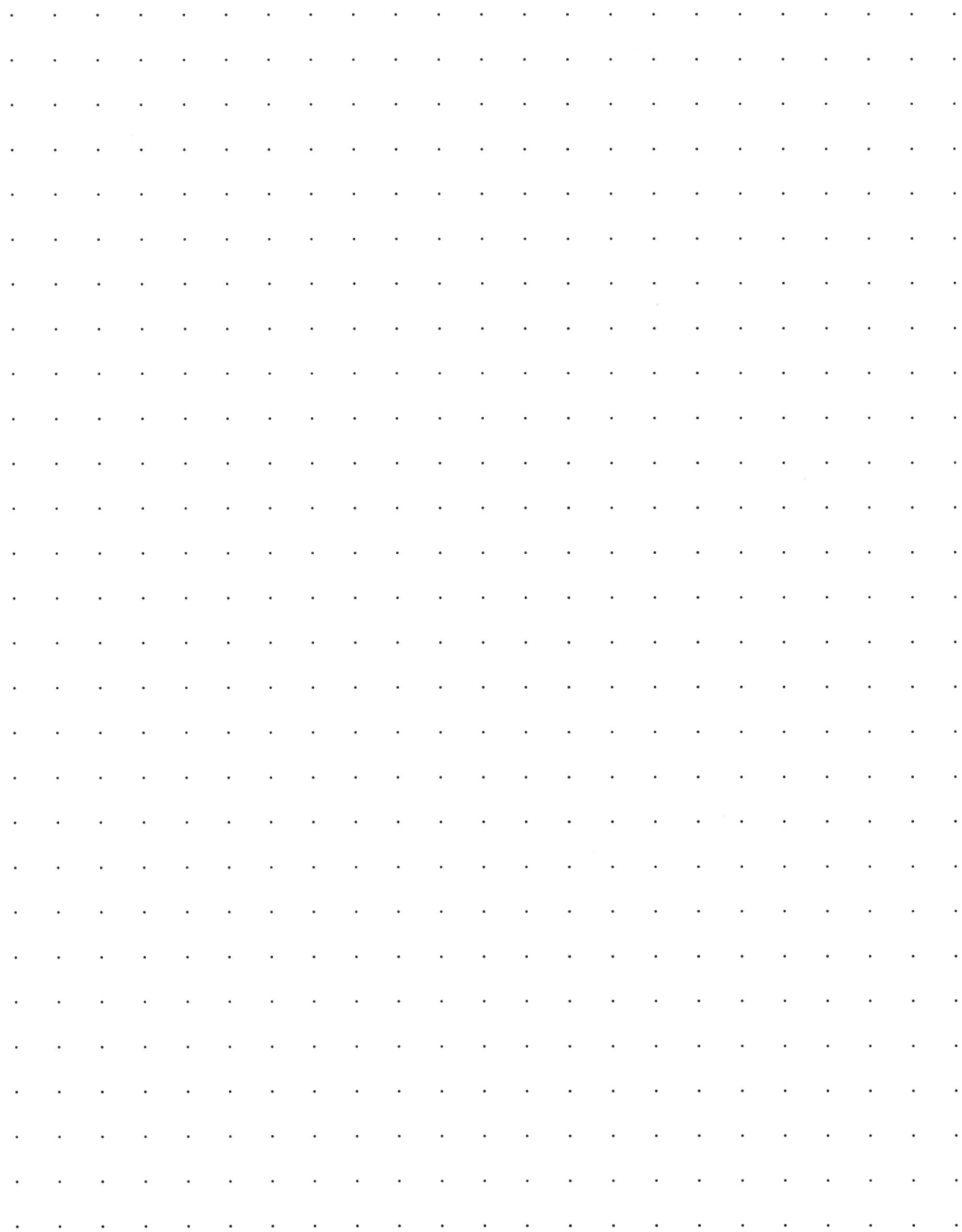

setting

Worldbuilding Basics: Setting

Description of your world:

Is there a main setting? If so, provide a brief description of this specific place:

What's the climate?

Details make the world feel more complete. Get in-depth about your setting and note any important sensory details:

What's the style of architecture?

Are there any important landmarks?

Worldbuilding Basics: Culture

What is the main culture like?

What values are important in this society?

Are there any subcultures relevant to the plot?

Describe how these subcultures differ the main culture:

How many people live in this world?

How big is your main town/city?

Worldbuilding Basics: Culture

Are there religions? If so, what are they?

Where do people worship? How do they worship?

What position do they have in both the society and the plot?

How do people dress?

What type of food do your characters eat?

What are some popular dishes or restaurants?

Worldbuilding Basics: Culture

What do people do for fun?

What are popular hobbies?

What is the government structure?

What is the political climate?

What is the economic structure?

How do the upper classes live?

How do the lower classes live?

Worldbuilding Basics: Magic & Tech

Is there magic?

If so, what type? How does it work?

What level of technology exists in this world?

Is this important to the plot somehow?

How can you incorporate technology into your story to make the world feel real?

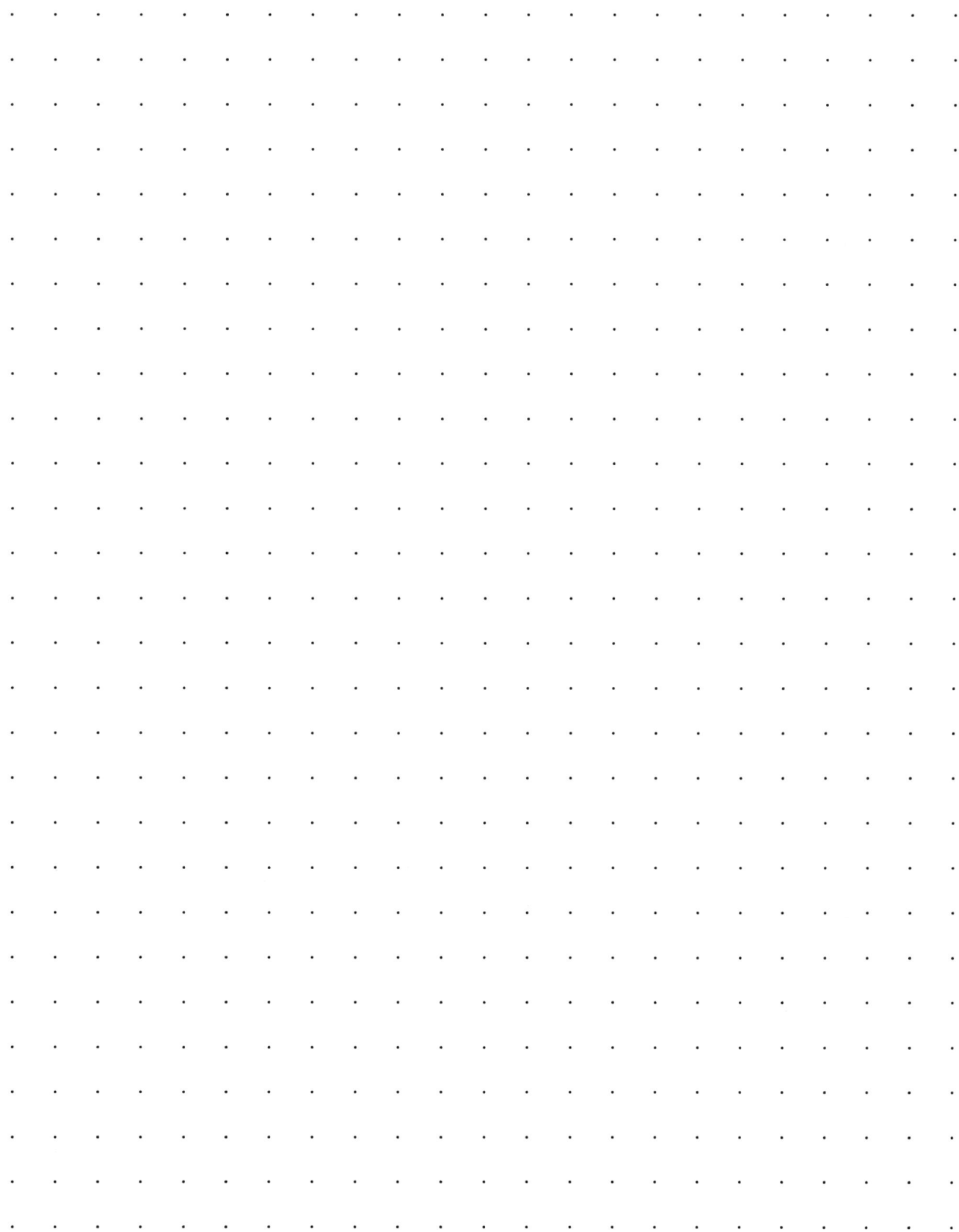

Location List

Location Name:

Relevance to Story:

Description:

Location Name:

Relevance to Story:

Description:

Location Name:

Relevance to Story:

Description:

Location Name:

Relevance to Story:

Description:

Location Name:

Relevance to Story:

Description:

Location Name:

Relevance to Story:

Description:

Location List

Location Name:	Description:
Relevance to Story:	

Location Name:	Description:
Relevance to Story:	

Location Name:	Description:
Relevance to Story:	

Location Name:	Description:
Relevance to Story:	

Location Name:	Description:
Relevance to Story:	

Location Name:	Description:
Relevance to Story:	

Location List

Location Name:	Description:
Relevance to Story:	

Location Name:	Description:
Relevance to Story:	

Location Name:	Description:
Relevance to Story:	

Location Name:	Description:
Relevance to Story:	

Location Name:	Description:
Relevance to Story:	

Location Name:	Description:
Relevance to Story:	

Location List

Location Name:

Relevance to Story:

Description:

Location Name:

Relevance to Story:

Description:

Location Name:

Relevance to Story:

Description:

Location Name:

Relevance to Story:

Description:

Location Name:

Relevance to Story:

Description:

Location Name:

Relevance to Story:

Description:

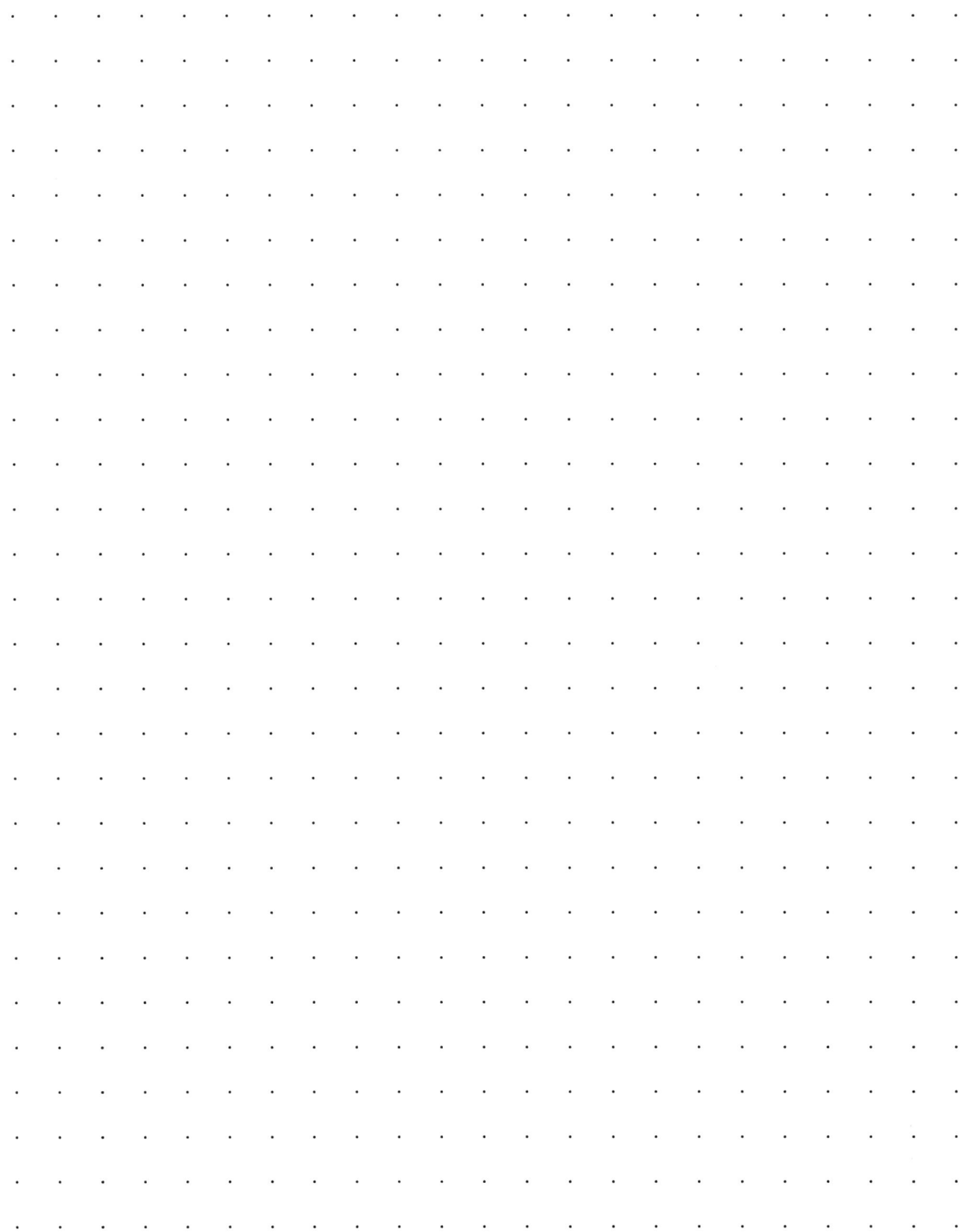

plot

Plot Summary

Write a brief summary of your overall story:

Who is the main character(s)? What is their motivation?

Who is the main antagonist(s)? What is their motivation?

Where does the story take place?

Plot Summary

What are the major themes of your story?

How will you establish these themes?

How will your character(s) change over the course of the story?

What are some of the lessons they learn?

Plot Basics: The Beginning

How does the story begin? If you're stuck, think about the main character's normal life.

What does your main character want at the beginning of the story?

Why do they want this?

What's stopping them from getting it?

Plot Basics: The Inciting Incident

What is the inciting incident, or the event that kicks off your character's journey?

What problem is the character(s) trying to solve?

Does your character's motivation/goal change after the inciting incident?

What's at stake if the character doesn't reach their goal?

Plot Basics: The Messy Middle

What major roadblocks does your character have to confront during their quest? List them out here.

Do you have any subplots? If so, list them out. Use the dot grid pages in this section to map out some of these conflicts if you need extra space.

Plot Basics: The Messy Middle

What is the midpoint crisis? This is where your character(s) is at their lowest before reaffirming their goal before the climax.

How does this impact their goal?

What changes after this point?

How does the character reaffirm their goal to move forward toward the climax?

Plot Basics: The Climax

What is the climax of your story?

What is the outcome of this finale?

Does the character reach their goal? If not, what does the character lose?

Plot Basics: The Resolution

How does your story end?

Can you connect the ending back to the beginning of the novel?

How does the ending connect back to your main theme(s)?

Plot Basics: Loose Ends

What loose ends will need to be tied up by the end of the draft?

If this is only the first book/story in a series, how will you leave this open-ended to hint at the next story?

research

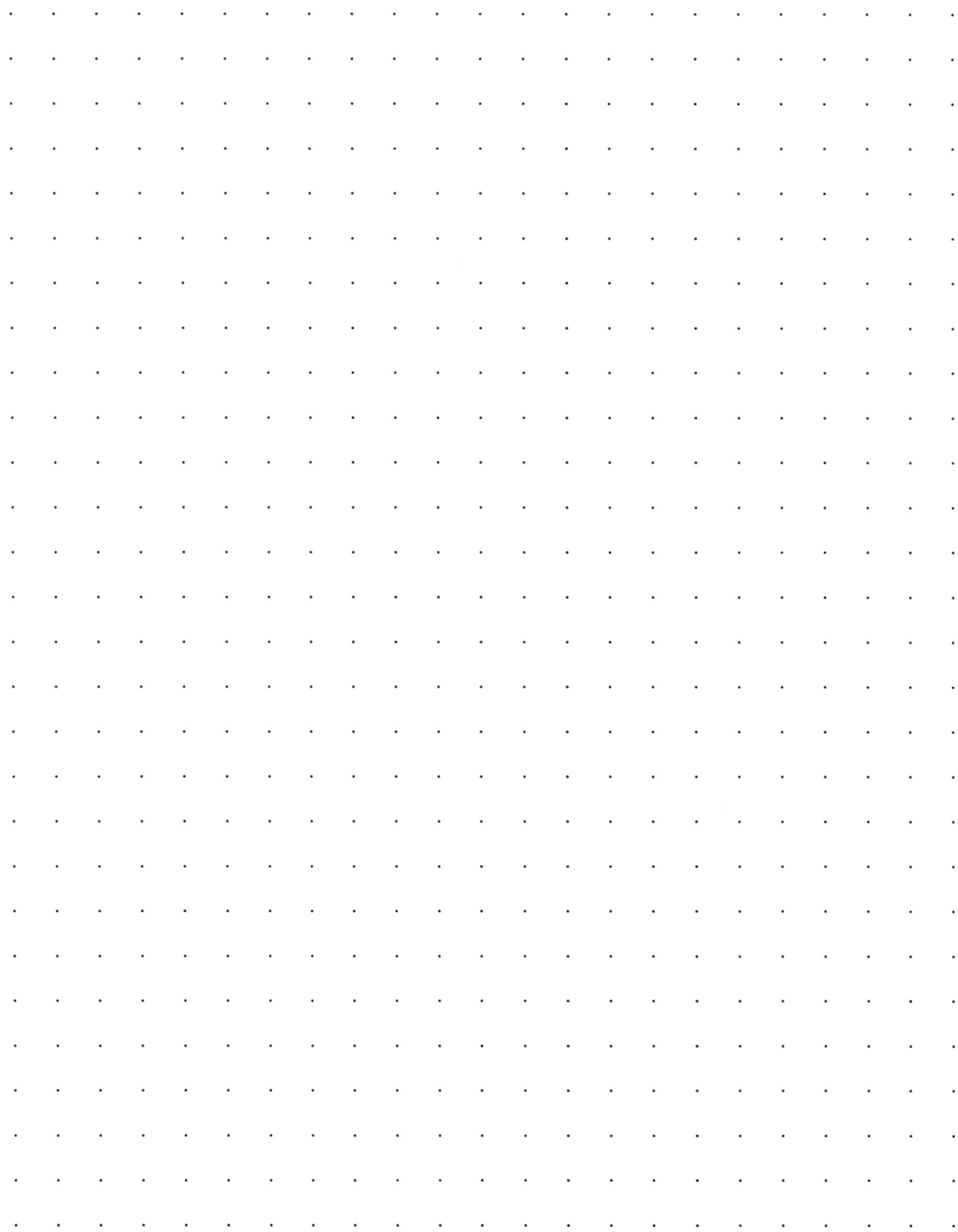

revisions

Quick Editing Tips

1. Even when you run an automatic spelling and grammar check, review each suggestion carefully. Computers don't understand the nuances of language!

2. If you can add "by zombies" to the end of your sentence and it still makes sense, you've written in passive voice. You may want to rewrite the sentence so the subject (usually the character) is doing the action. This is more engaging, especially in fiction. If you want to draw special attention to the action itself or take away the character's agency, then you might keep the sentence in passive voice.

3. If you have more than one character in a scene that use the same pronouns, it's better to be specific and descriptive. Use their names for clarity as appropriate. This ensures your readers understand exactly who is doing what thing in that scene.

4. Remember that you don't have to show every single action to explain every single scene transition. It's okay to cut out the boring details of walking back to someone's house and pick up the scene at that new location instead. This keeps your story moving right along.

5. When it comes to "show, don't tell," remember that you want to show emotions but tell feelings. It's fine to tell readers that a character is tired and leave it at that. But if a character is experiencing anxiety, describe the physical symptoms going along with that emotion to truly engage and immerse your reader.

6. Take a step back as needed for perspective. Editing is a long and tedious process, so take it slow and remember that you're human. You need breaks and time to rest.

Editing Checklist

- ○ Run a spell check on your entire document.

- ○ Remove double spaces after periods.

- ○ Rewrite sentences as needed for clear, concise wording.

- ○ Rewrite weak, passive sentences into active voice.

- ○ Check your verb tense to ensure consistency.

- ○ Check for unintentional repetitive sentences and/or statements.

- ○ Check your dialogue punctuation carefully.

- ○ Check that every sentence has ending punctuation.

- ○ Make sure paragraphs are properly indented.

- ○ Use consistent formatting, including consistent line spacing.

- ○ Remove cliches unless they're used purposefully in dialogue.

- ○ Delete any repeated scenes left over from revisions.

- ○ Vary your sentence structure for interest and flow.

- ○ Add or rewrite scene transitions to be clear and smooth.

- ○ Check that your point of view is always clear. Avoid head hops if you're writing from a limited perspective.

- ○ Delete any scenes that don't move your story forward.

- ○ Refer to each character clearly and avoid vague pronouns.

- ○ Remove as many instances of "that" as possible.

- ○ Rewrite instances of telling to showing (as appropriate).

- ○ Use contractions if it fits your style, especially in dialogue.

Important Words & Phrases In Your Story

Important Words & Phrases In Your Story

First Round of Revisions

Date started: _____   Date completed: _____

Beginning word count: _____   Ending word count: _____

Next draft due by: _____   Next draft word goal: _____

Due to betas? ◯ Yes ◯ No   Due to betas by: _____

Due to editor? ◯ Yes ◯ No   Due to editor by: _____

Major plot changes:

Major character arc changes:

Other notes:

Second Round of Revisions

Date started: _____   Date completed: _____

Beginning word count: _____   Ending word count: _____

Next draft due by: _____   Next draft word goal: _____

Due to betas? ◯ Yes ◯ No   Due to betas by: _____

Due to editor? ◯ Yes ◯ No   Due to editor by: _____

Major plot changes:

Major character arc changes:

Other notes:

Notes

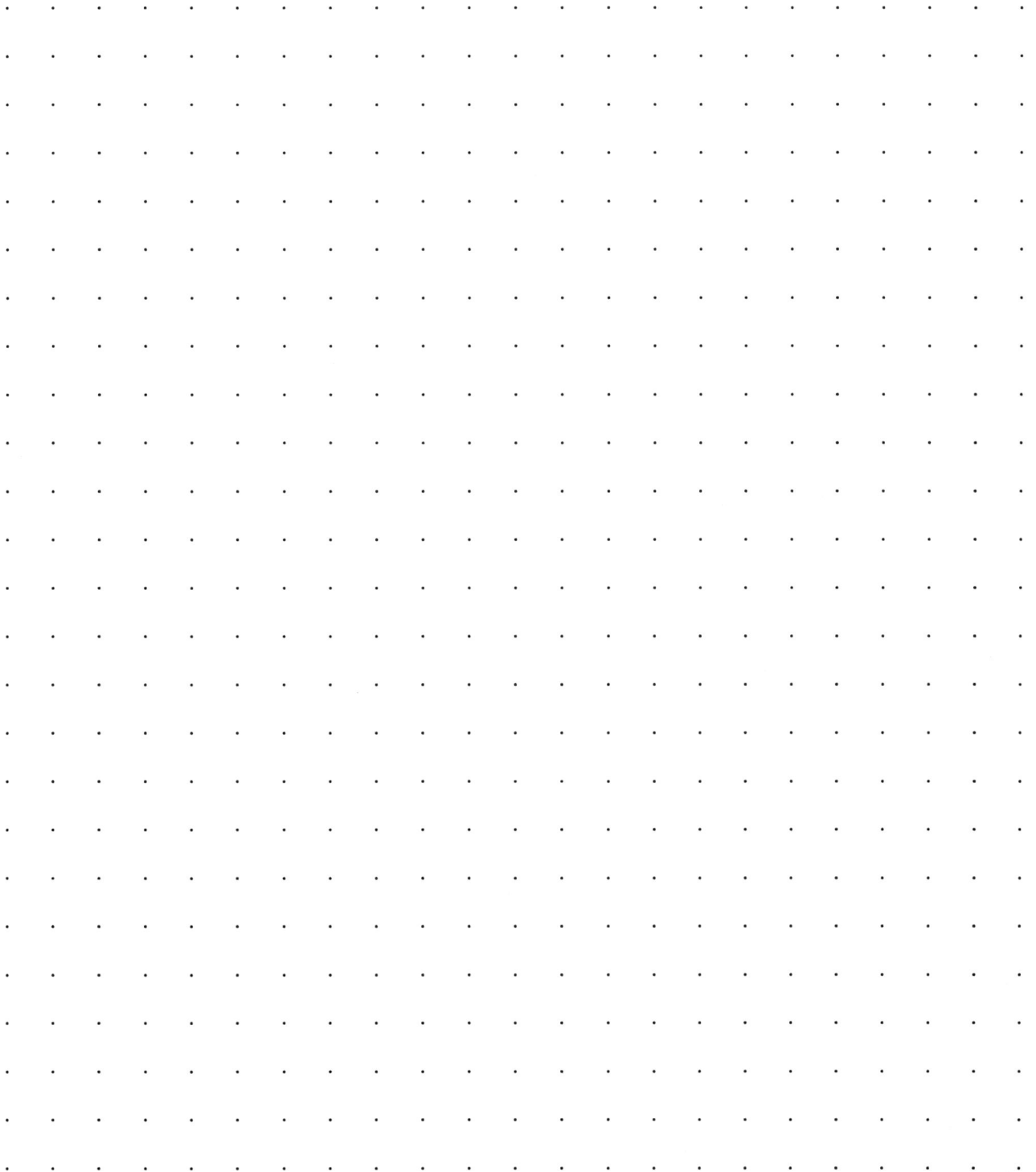

Notes

Third Round of Revisions

Date started: _____   Date completed: _____

Beginning word count: _____   Ending word count: _____

Next draft due by: _____   Next draft word goal: _____

Due to betas? ◯ Yes ◯ No   Due to betas by: _____

Due to editor? ◯ Yes ◯ No   Due to editor by: _____

Major plot changes:

Major character arc changes:

Other notes:

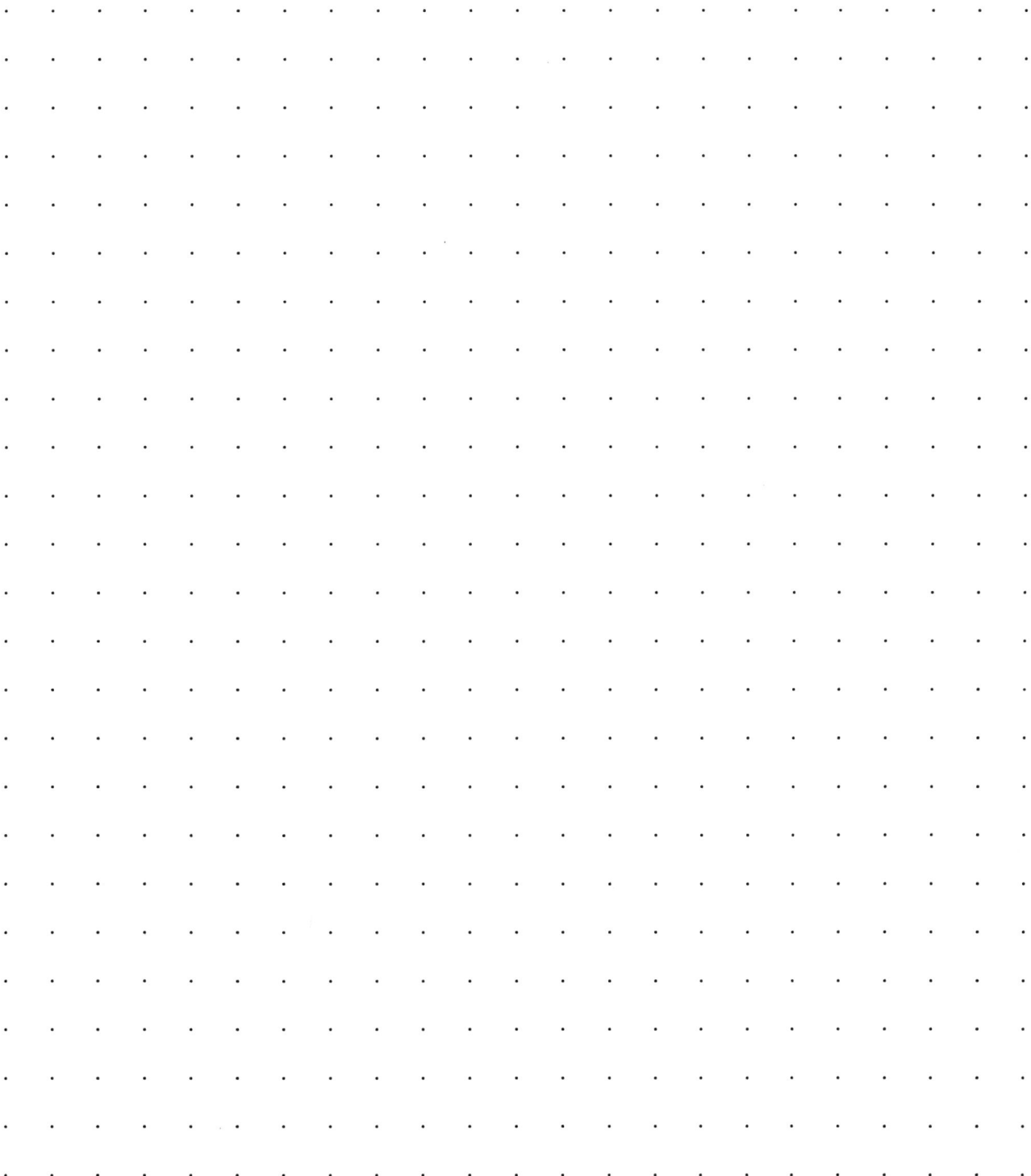

Notes

Fourth Round of Revisions

Date started: _____   Date completed: _____

Beginning word count: _____   Ending word count: _____

Next draft due by: _____   Next draft word goal: _____

Due to betas? ○ Yes ○ No   Due to betas by: _____

Due to editor? ○ Yes ○ No   Due to editor by: _____

Major plot changes:

Major character arc changes:

Other notes:

Notes

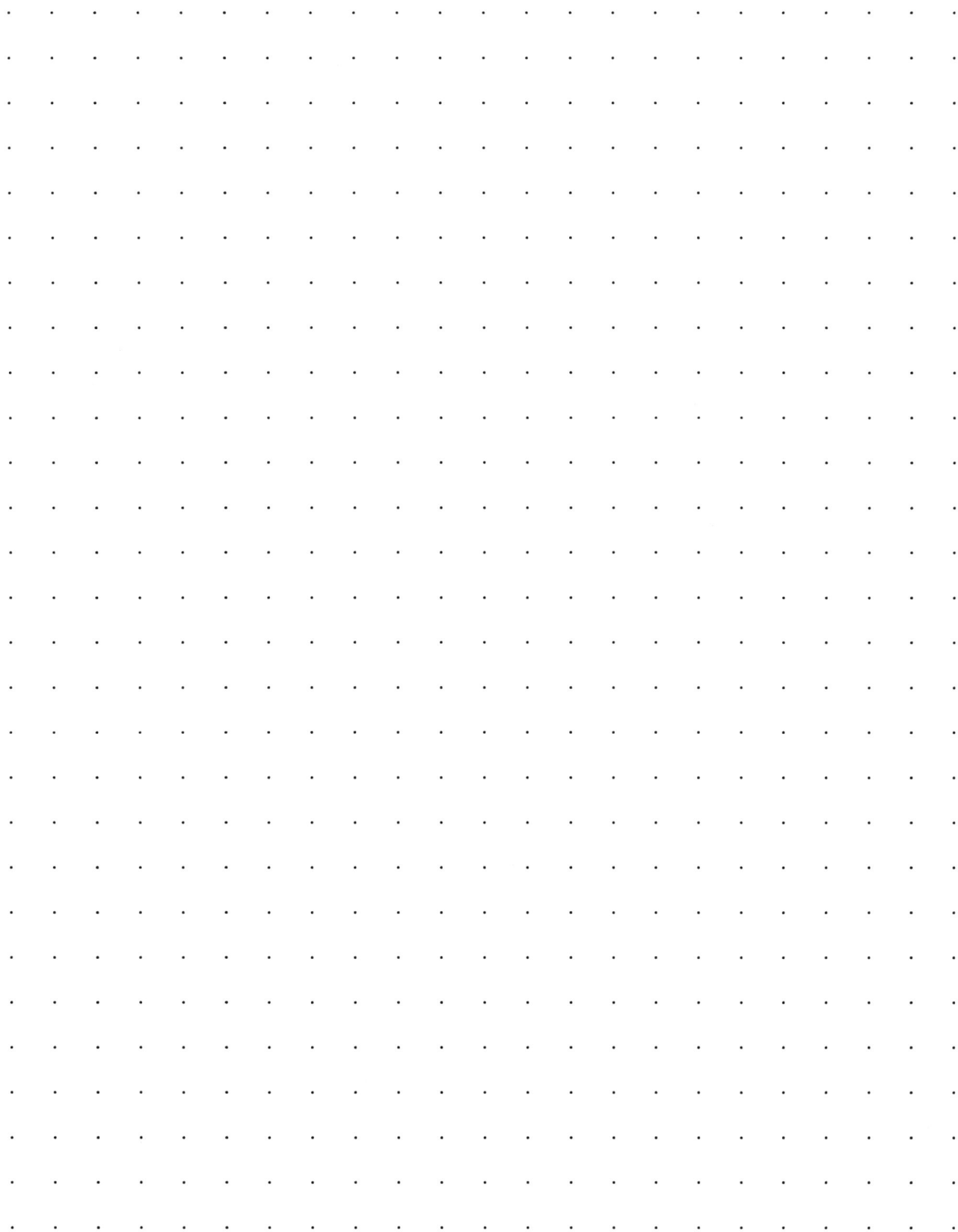

www.ingramcontent.com/pod-product-compliance
Lightning Source LLC
Chambersburg PA
CBHW061756260326
41914CB00006B/1130